PAST & PRESENT

HILLSBORO

OPPOSITE: The Pacific Northwest Clay Works, owned by James Henry Sewell, was on the south side of Evergreen Road at its intersection with Sewell Avenue, which was named after James Henry. In this 1891 photograph, fire-hardened pipe sections are shown in stacks. The clay works supplied much of Oregon with drainage pipes. By 1903, the clay works had a national clientele. (Five Oaks Museum, WCM 1,171)

HILLSBORO

Arthur Sommers

Library of Congress Control Number: 2022944859

Published by Arcadia Publishing
Charleston, South Carolina

Printed in the United States of America

For all general information, please contact Arcadia Publishing:
Telephone 843-853-2070
Fax 843-853-0044
E-mail sales@arcadiapublishing.com
For customer service and orders:
Toll-Free 1-888-313-2665

Visit us on the Internet at www.arcadiapublishing.com

ON THE FRONT COVER: The Commercial Hotel sits on the northwest corner of Second Avenue and Washington Street. A livery stable is across Second Avenue from the hotel. Stables were often located near hotels to provide care for the guests' horses. This hotel burned down in January 1912 due to a fire caused by two young boys playing with matches. The brightly colored Hillsboro Artists' Regional Theatre (HART) is now on the corner where the Commercial Hotel once sat. Both photographs are looking north up Second Avenue. (Past, Five Oaks Museum; present, photograph by the author.)

ON THE BACK COVER: This Oregon Electric Railway train has stopped at the Orenco ticket and freight station. Orenco was once an independent incorporated city just east of Hillsboro. The city had financial problems during the Great Depression after the local nursery company folded, and the city disincorporated in 1938. The City of Hillsboro eventually annexed the Orenco area, which is centered on the intersection of Cornell Road and Century Boulevard. (Five Oaks Museum.)

CONTENTS

ACKNOWLEDGMENTS

Unless otherwise indicated, the black-and-white photographs—representing the "past"—appear courtesy of the Five Oaks Museum, formerly known as the Washington County Museum. The museum's unique photograph locator numbers (written as "WCM" followed by the image's locator number) are shown at the end of captions. The modern photographs—representing the "present"—were taken by the author during the early months of 2022 unless otherwise indicated.

Sanborn Insurance maps of Hillsboro from 1884, 1888, 1892, 1902, 1912, and 1921 were used to confirm the locations of many of the buildings featured in this book. Hillsboro's north–south roads used to be called streets, but by the time of the 1921 Sanborn map, the north–south streets had been redesignated as avenues. Regardless of what era a photograph is from, the author uses "avenue" when referring to numbered roadway names.

Another source used in research was the University of Oregon's Historic Oregon Newspapers site at oregonnews.uoregon.edu.

Judy Goldmann, a lifelong resident of Hillsboro and a member of the Hillsboro Historical Society, provided a wealth of research materials, reviewed early drafts of the manuscript, and suggested needed corrections and improvements. Goldmann is a descendant of Joe Meek, an early Washington County pioneer.

Victoria Sundell, Mariah Berlanga-Shevchuk, Debera Knox, and Dennis Trune of the Five Oaks Museum were all instrumental in helping with the creation of this book. Carol Reich, library manager at the Hillsboro Public Library, helped identify street addresses using the library's old city directories.

The author is donating all royalties to the Five Oaks Museum.

Errors in the book are the sole responsibility of the author.

Introduction

From the area's agricultural beginnings to the high-tech prowess displayed in the modern era, the people of Hillsboro have led the way in Oregon and beyond. Hillsboro is the fifth-largest city in Oregon, and its current population trends younger and more ethnically diverse and is more involved in the workforce than the rest of the state. An estimated 104,670 residents called the city home in 2022. Thousands more commute in for work, visit for cultural events, and hold historic ties to the region. It has always been the people who make Hillsboro a special place to live.

From Indigenous stewardship to habitat restoration, people have shaped Hillsboro's natural environment into a pleasant and healthy place. Hillsboro sits in the center of the Tualatin Valley in northwest Oregon. Low, forested mountains mark every horizon. Shaped by glacial floods some 15,000 years ago, this valley is naturally marshy and wet.

The Tualatin Kalapuya (also called Atfalati) have called this land home since time immemorial. The tribe is the namesake of both the valley and its meandering river. For centuries prior to their forced removal, Kalapuyans engineered lush oak savannas across the valley through controlled burns and thoughtful harvesting. This Indigenous land stewardship was essential in creating the parklike environment and rich soil so foundational to the European settlements that arose in the area. Today, Kalapuya descendants belong to the Confederated Tribes of Grand Ronde.

The people who arrived in the 19th century destroyed 95 percent of Oregon's oak savanna through rampant mismanagement and prohibition of Indigenous controlled burns. For decades, they dumped sewage and cannery waste into the wetlands and logged ancient forests without consideration for the future. Since the 1960s, ongoing efforts by Hillsboro residents have led to organized funding and education meant to restore these important natural habitats. Today, Hillsboro's Jackson Bottom Wetland is a nature preserve home to native plants and migratory birds. Orenco Nature Park holds a portion of oak savanna, and Noble Woods contains majestic old cedar and fir trees.

Tenacity, leadership, and community spirit brought Hillsboro's early non-Indigenous residents together. In 1840, mountain men Joseph Meek, Robert Newell, and a few others retired from fur trapping and established homesteads in the West Union area in today's north Hillsboro. At the time, Britain's Hudson's Bay Company dominated the Pacific Northwest through fur trapping and lumber export. The mountain men, along with their Indigenous Nez Perce wives and young children, survived a harsh and wet winter by living in bark huts. Their tenacity cemented the East Tualatin Plains as a destination for new arrivals headed westward across the country.

From the 1840s to 1860s, mass migration on the Oregon Trail changed power dynamics and land use in the Pacific Northwest. The opportunity for land ownership, a belief in manifest destiny, and—for some—a new start beyond financial debt and a slavery-based society, enticed thousands of people to make the grueling wagon journey west. The 1850 Donation Land Claim Act, which gave white married couples 640 acres, drove further migration.

Hillsboro benefited from strong leaders. Along with newcomer David Hill, the previously mentioned mountain men launched Oregon's provisional government in 1843. They governed the Tuality District from a cabin on Hill's property.

In addition to showing tenacity and leadership, Hillsboro's early non-Indigenous residents developed close-knit community ties. Thanks to the quality soil and open plains created by the Kalapuya, the new arrivals quickly established family farms. Hill sold a portion of his land claim to one little farming town, which was named Hillsborough in his honor. Numerous small communities, such as Hillsboro, Farmington, and Helvetia, provided churches, one-room schoolhouses, and grange halls. Surviving buildings from these early years include the 1874 Hillsboro Grange (page 24) and the 1866 Imbrie house (page 71).

Through the end of the 19th century, Hillsboro residents labored to build the city's agricultural economy and civic services. In the 1890s, Hillsboro's 1,200 residents transformed a village into a lively town. They milled flour and lumber next to the railroad tracks just south of Main Street and transported dairy to Portland by steamboats on the Tualatin River. Portland grew into a major port city partly because of Hillsboro's farmers and mill workers.

A new post office officially shortened the town's name to Hillsboro in 1892. The city mandated fire-resistant brick (instead of wood) buildings downtown and formed the fire department, water, and electricity systems. Popular cultural activities included brass bands, fraternal societies, the annual stallion show, and four rowdy downtown saloons. Later, two interurban electric trains propelled commercial growth: the Oregon Electric Railway on Washington Street and the Red Electric on Main Street. The 1888 First National Bank building (page 22) and the 1890 Building (page 17) still stand downtown.

Growth continued beyond downtown. Wealthy businessmen Simon Gannett Reed and William Ladd ran a large horse farm that became today's Reedville and South Hillsboro neighborhoods. Shute Park, a brickyard that was turned into the city's first park, was home to a roller rink, county fair, and infantry drill grounds. The first standalone Hillsboro High School was built in 1913. Hungarian immigrants populated Orenco, a company town for Oregon Nursery Company employees, which Hillsboro acquired after the company folded during the Great Depression. Japanese families established berry farms, and a few African Americans braved Oregon's Black Exclusion laws to settle in Helvetia. Barred from land ownership, Chinese men frequently cleared stumps for Hillsboro farm fields, and Indigenous people traveled off the reservation for harvest work. Today, the Orenco neighborhood and the 1916 Iwasaki Bros farm help to represent the role of immigrant and minority laborers in the development of Hillsboro.

During the Great Depression, the WPA built the Sunset Highway, and Hillsboro purchased Dr. Elmer Smith's airfield, which became the Hillsboro Airport. In the World War II era, injustices impacted agriculture, as the United States trucked in Mexican migrant laborers (known as braceros) and incarcerated Japanese families. Food processing surpassed agriculture, including at places like the Carnation Condensed Milk plant (page 76) in downtown Hillsboro.

After being changed by the war, people transformed Hillsboro into a major culture and technology hub. Tektronix in neighboring Beaverton planted the seeds for the Silicon Forest. This network of tech companies in the Tualatin Valley includes Intel's 1979 Hawthorne Farm and 1994 Ronler Acres facilities. Hillsboro rapidly expanded into a global tech and manufacturing hub. An influx of new residents, including immigrants from around the world, prompted the annexation of Tanasbourne in 1987 and South Hillsboro in 2015, as well as the development of Orenco and Amberglen as transit-connected neighborhoods in 1997 and 2010, respectively. The culturally diverse community flourishes during annual festivals, through local restaurants, and at performances at the Walters Cultural Arts Center (page 26).

As Hillsboro grew from a farm village to a high-tech city, its residents designed structures and places to help the community thrive. Every landscape and building has people's labor, dreams, and stories behind it. May the memories of the city they built make you imagine their lives, value their efforts, and recognize that you play a role in shaping the future of Hillsboro.

—Victoria Sundell
Head of Integrated Learning, Five Oaks Museum

CHAPTER 1

Scenes along Main Street

This is a mid-19th-century view looking west down Main Street from its intersection with Third Avenue. The two-story Tualatin Hotel is on the right. The trees in front of the hotel are used as a reference point in many old images of Main Street. On the left, a small group of men are standing on the sidewalk in front of the Farmers Exchange building. (WCM 904.)

The Tualatin Hotel had a distinctive round sign advertising its presence. It is said to be the first hotel in Hillsboro, having been built in 1852. The hotel was bought by the Weil family and torn down. They constructed a large building on the site in 1919 to house their department store. (Above, author's collection; below, WCM 249.)

The Weil Department Store building was remodeled in 1966 to house many different businesses. The name of the building was changed to Weil Arcade, with street addresses of 229–235 E. Main Street. The above photograph was taken in June 2021.

The Weil Arcade suffered a devastating arson fire on January 2, 2022. The below photograph, showing some of the fire damage, was taken on January 9, 2022. The entire damaged structure was demolished in the summer of 2022.

The above photograph shows the southeast corner of the brick courthouse built in 1873, which replaced a small wood-frame courthouse in the same location. The front entrance to the courthouse originally faced Main Street. It was not until the current courthouse was built in 1928 that the front entrance was oriented to face Second Avenue. In the modern photograph, the trees to the left are giant sequoias planted by John Porter in 1880, when the courthouse entrance led to Main Street. The modern photograph shows the southeast corner of the new courthouse. (Past, WCM 15,917.)

In the 1900 photograph below, crowds gather during a fair held on Main Street. The buildings on the left are on the south side of Main Street. The small two-story building at far left was the county courthouse built in 1852 on the courthouse square. The 1852 wood-frame courthouse was moved to this spot on Main Street to make way for the 1873 construction of a brick courthouse (see page 14). The buildings on the south side of Main Street in the modern image are completely different. (Past, WCM 599.)

The western corner of Hillsboro National Bank on Main Street is on the left below. On the right, across Second Avenue, is the building that has become known as the 1890 Building. Hillsboro National Bank was replaced by the Hillsboro branch of US Bank. That Hillsboro branch—and many other US Bank branches in Washington County—closed in November 2021. The 1890 Building appears in both images. (Past, Oregon Historical Society.)

The above photograph was taken in 1912 and shows the 1890 Building on the southwest corner of Second Avenue and Main Street. Below is the same building in 2022. (Past, WCM 19,097.)

A J.C. Penney store opened in 1930 at 230 E. Main Street. Now, the building houses a few small businesses. These were affected by the Weil Arcade fire on January 2, 2022, because the street and sidewalks were closed. The street and sidewalk on the south side were reopened in March 2022. (Past, WCM 14,180.)

The Hillsboro Montgomery Ward, at far right below, had the address of 303 E. Main Street according to the 1959 city directory. Montgomery Ward was a catalog store; it and the Tots to Teens store on the corner were both short-lived at their Main Street locations. Washington Federal Savings and Loan is at far left, with the Peoples Bank across Third Avenue on the southwest corner. The Peoples Bank was originally Shute's 1911 bank building. (Past, author's collection.)

Street Scene Hillsboro Oregon

Smith P785

The *Hillsboro Argus* newspaper had its business office and print plant at 250 E. Main Street from 1917 to 1955. Below, a 1950s parade is passing in front of the office. The *Argus* relocated in 1955 to 150 SE Third Avenue, which was its last operating location. The *Argus* location on Main Street is now home to the Thai House restaurant. (Past, WCM 12,808.)

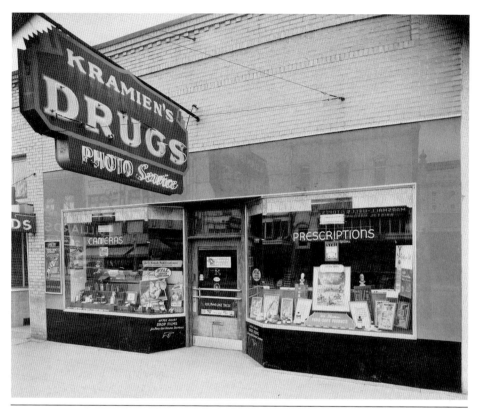

Kramien's Drugs was at 256 E. Main Street for many years after World War II. The owners of many drugstores and banks chose Main Street as a desirable place from which to operate. Today, the Kramien's building is occupied by Gimre's Shoes. The sign hanging over the sidewalk has been replaced with a sign that sits flush against the building. (Past, WCM 14,135.)

This narrow building was the site of John Wright Shute's First National Bank, which was founded in 1888. He sold the building at 253 E. Main Street to a man who converted it into a theater by 1911. The movie theater assumed the name Venetian in 1927 and at one time was also called the Town. The narrow building and the adjacent space have recently been converted into a restaurant called the Venetian. (Past, WCM 19,462.)

In 1911, John Wright Shute built his second bank on Main Street—the American National Bank. Shute's 1911 bank building now houses the Bennett Urban Farm Store at 276 E. Main Street. Streets on the west side of First Avenue carry the "west" (or "W") identifier, and streets east of First Avenue carry the "east" (or "E") identifier. The shield at top of the bank's front reads "1911." (Past, author's collection.)

The Hillsboro Grange hosted a convention in 1891 at the group's meeting hall on Main Street. The front of the building has changed little over the years, although the wooden porch on the second floor has been removed. This building is at 263 E. Main Street. The Hillsboro Grange has met at 245 SE Third Avenue since the 1930s (see page 43). (Past, WCM 675.)

The Independent Order of Odd Fellows had a meeting hall at the northwest corner of Third Avenue and Main Street. The building burned down in 1894, and the Odd Fellows built a new hall in 1898 on the same corner at 267 E. Main Street. (Past, WCM 871.)

Trinity Lutheran Church on Main Street was dedicated in May 1949. The following year, a new sanctuary was constructed at the west end of the building, with more additions built later. In the late 1990s, the congregation relocated, and the city bought the church property on Main Street. The building is now known as the Glen and Viola Walters Cultural Arts Center at 527 E. Main Street. (Past, WCM 12,431.)

A fire destroyed the home at 545 E. Main Street in March 1987. This house was built in 1908 adjacent to the east end of Trinity Lutheran Church. After the fire, the lot remained empty for almost two decades. In 2005, the empty lot became home to the Hillsboro Rotary Club Centennial Park. The house at 557 E. Main Street, which is visible at right below, is now just barely visible through the magnolia trees. (Past, author's collection.)

A temperature and time sign juts out from the corner of the Washington Federal Savings & Loan building at the southeast corner of Third Avenue and Main Street. This corner used to be occupied by the Washington Hotel, which was demolished in 1956 to make room for construction of the bank building. Heritage Bank moved into the Washington Federal building after some remodeling and the removal of the sign. (Past, WCM 14,365.)

The First National Bank building at 350 E. Main Street is visible at right in these images looking east along the southern part of Main Street. Almost hidden behind it is the post office building erected by the WPA during the Great Depression. Farther down the street is the steeple of the First Congregational Church. The Vault Theater at 350 E. Main Street is so named because it occupies the old First National Bank building. The theater is home to Bag & Baggage Productions, a professional theater group. (Past, author's collection.)

The WPA post office at 372 E. Main Street is shown above. The building was erected in 1935 and torn down in 1978, and the post office moved to its present location on the southwest corner of First Avenue and Main Street. A four-story apartment complex now sits on the old post office lot. (Past, author's collection.)

CHAPTER 2

SCENES ALONG OTHER STREETS

The "Photo Gallery" sign is sticking out from the front of a small wood-frame building on Second Avenue. This was one of three photograph studios on Second Avenue within just a few blocks of each other on the same side of the street. The view is looking north up Second Avenue toward its intersection with Washington Street. An earlier view of this block can be seen on page 85. In this image, many of the empty lots have been filled in with new businesses in new buildings. (Author's collection.)

In these images looking north along Second Avenue, most of the buildings on the west (left) side of the street are still there, as seen in the early 1950s image below. The trees on the left were planted on the courthouse square. It is hard to miss that the giant sequoias, which are now visible over the top of the building, have grown much taller during the intervening years. (Past, author's collection.)

Street Scene - Hillsboro Oregon

SCENES ALONG OTHER STREETS

These two views look south down Second Avenue from its intersection with Main Street. The 1890 Building is on the right, with the Pythian Building a few doors down on the same side of the street. A photographer named Christian took the above picture in the 1950s. Below, the trees on the right indicate where the Pythian Building is located. (Past, author's collection.)

The second floor of the Pythian Building has not changed much over the years, although the occupants of the first floor have changed often. The Knights of Pythias emblem at the top of the front facade indicates that this has been the meeting hall for lodge No. 34 since 1909. The building uses the street addresses of 145 and 147 SE Second Avenue. (Past, WCM 14,490.)

Wiley's Place was at 142 SE Second Avenue on the eastern side, across the street from the Pythian Building. The saloon was often simply referred to as Wiley's, but its official name was Wiley's Place. It was torn down in 1969. In the modern image, a young lady is standing on the sidewalk in front of where Wiley's was once located. The space is now a large parking lot that temporarily hosts a beer garden and food truck. (Past, WCM 1,154.)

The Masonic Hall on the southeast corner of Second Avenue and Lincoln Street looks essentially the same after all these years. Before this structure was built in 1925 at 176 NE Second Avenue, the Masons met at different halls around the city. In 1884, one hall was at the northeast corner of Second Avenue and Main Street. (Past, WCM 756.)

PUBLIC LIBRARY.
HILLSBORO. OREGON.

A Carnegie library was built at 209 Lincoln Street in 1914. Steel tycoon Andrew Carnegie funded the construction of more than 2,000 libraries across the nation. The building is still there but no longer houses the city's library, which moved to its Shute Park location in 1975. Numerous small businesses now reside in the old library building, including the Syun Japanese restaurant, which has an outside dining area. The main city library is now on Brookwood Parkway. (Past, author's collection.)

The three round emblems on this building's wall just below the roofline are medical caduceus symbols. The building at 150 NE Third Avenue was originally an office for a group of three physicians in the 1950s. The doctors' names were Kabeiseman, Hutchenson, and Pitman. By the 1960s, they had relocated to a medical clinic at 660 E. Baseline Street. This building on Third Avenue now houses a DUI evaluation clinic. (Past, WCM 14,410.)

SCENES ALONG OTHER STREETS

The two-story building on the corner of Second Avenue and Washington Street was erected in 1891. It had an address of 205 SE Second Avenue. It housed City Hall and the city's fire department, and the Masons met upstairs. The large roll-up doors at the far left corner were for the fire trucks. The Oregon Electric Railway tracks on Washington Street are visible near the bottom below. This corner is now occupied by City Center Apartments. (Past, WCM 560.)

This Quonset hut–style building was erected in 1921 on the grounds of Shute Park. It was just off Maple Street where it is intersected by Ninth Avenue. The structure was called the Pavilion and was famous for holding dances, and was also used as a roller rink. It was torn down in 1974, and the space is now occupied by a playground. At one time, there was a baseball field north of Shute Park just across Maple Street. The Shute Aquatic Center is now where the baseball field used to be. (Past, WCM 12,439.)

Shute Park   Hillsboro, Oreg.

There is a large curve in Tenth Avenue as the roadway transitions from running east–west to north–south. The tree line at left is the eastern boundary of Shute Park. The isolated homes across the street have been replaced with modern apartment complexes and small business offices. The old dirt road is now a wide paved road with four lanes and a median. (Past, WCM 908.)

Scores of schoolchildren are waiting for a special excursion train to take them to Forest Grove for the 1913 county fair. They are standing along the Oregon Electric Railway tracks in front of the ticket station. In the distance is the steeple above the front entrance to the United Methodist Church on the northwest corner of Third Avenue and Washington Street. A parking lot for the Faber building now occupies the corner where the church once stood. (Past, WCM 1,601.)

SCENES ALONG OTHER STREETS

In 1933, the Hillsboro Grange moved from Main Street (see page 24) to this building at 245 SE Third Avenue. As in many of the other modern images in this book, the present view of the Grange building is mostly obscured by the tree that was planted at the front door. (Past, WCM 12,864.)

Jones Hospital, at Seventh Avenue and Baseline Street, had 74 beds when this photograph was taken in the late 1940s. In 1955, the hospital was purchased for $210,000 and became Tuality Community Hospital. In subsequent years, remodeling and new construction resulted in the present complex of healthcare buildings covering three blocks in downtown Hillsboro, still centered on Seventh Avenue. It is now the Hillsboro Medical Center. (Past, WCM 12,423.)

Flowers have been placed upon a grave in the c. 1910 photograph above at the Pioneer Cemetery; before 1973, this burial ground consisted of three privately owned cemeteries adjacent to each other. In 1973, the city received the deeds for the cemetery land and assumed responsibility for maintenance of all three. The cemetery is at 1601 SW Baseline Street just before the road crosses the bridge over Dairy Creek. A grave marker for the city's namesake, David Hill, is seen below. (Past, WCM 3,884.)

Although 100 years separate these two photographs, the Orenco grocery store building looks essentially the same. The Orenco grocery store, drugstore, and hotel were built just south of the railroad tracks along Orenco's Main Street. The old Main Street is now called Alder Street. The grocery store was built in 1908. After it closed, it started to deteriorate. A couple bought it in 1983 and spent years restoring the building, which they completed in 1989 and then lived in. (Past, WCM 993.)

SCENES ALONG OTHER STREETS

Orenco Drug Co. had a large facade that was removed. The current building on Alder Street has a modern addition on the east side. The sloped roof is visible peeking out on both sides of the facade in the photograph at left. Above, the door leading out to the second-floor balcony has been removed. (Past, WCM 073.)

On the northwestern border of the Hillsboro city limits is a grove of oak trees called Five Oaks, which served as a meeting place for the local Atfalati Indigenous peoples and was later used in the same manner by European Americans who arrived in the area. Only one of the original oaks still stands, while new oak trees were planted to replicate the original grouping. The trees are in the Sunset Highway Business Park at Casper Court and Clark Lane. (Past, WCM 19,151.)

CHAPTER

3

SCHOOLS AND
CHURCHES

This 1879 photograph shows three school buildings that were erected at different times on the northwest corner of Third Avenue and Baseline Street. The small building at far left was constructed in 1854 and housed the first school in the city of Hillsboro; it is not to be confused with the one-room log cabin in West Union that was the first dedicated school building in Washington County. The structure in the center was erected later, and the larger two-story schoolhouse was the last to be built. All three buildings went up in flames in 1889. (WCM 1,213.)

Burt William Barnes introduced high school classes to Hillsboro in 1904. The 1906 photograph above shows that year's graduating class, which consisted of only freshmen and sophomores, as there were no juniors or seniors yet. The first four-year class did not graduate until 1908. The photograph below shows the 2021 graduating class of Hillsboro High School, which had a senior class of 311, with 252 who graduated. The students are observing the COVID-19 pandemic social-distancing guidelines. (Past, WCM 15,622; present, Hillsboro School District.)

SCHOOLS AND CHURCHES

An increasing student population in Hillsboro required a large new high school, so in 1928, one was built at 645 NE Lincoln Street on the corner of Lincoln Street and Sixth Avenue. The Art Deco building was designed by F. Marion Stokes. It was demolished in 2009. The J.B. Thomas sports field now occupies the site at the western end of the block, and Lincoln Street Elementary School is at the eastern end. (Past, WCM 13,061.)

Originally, this school consisted of just the front half of the building, with its front entrance facing Oak Street. The back half was added later. In 1929, the school started being called David Hill Elementary School. Its property took up the entire block bordered by Fourth and Fifth Avenues and Oak and Fir Streets (Fir Street is now Walnut Street). The school closed in 2009. Today, the Miller Education Center's alternative schools at 440 and 472 Oak Street occupy the space. (Past, author's collection.)

NO 15 HIGH SCHOOL BLDG HILLSBORO ORE

Tualatin Valley Presbyterians worship at the Old Scotch Church, which was founded in 1873 and is located at 30865 Scotch Church Road. The above photograph shows the 1960 dedication ceremony for the church additions that were completed that year. The building was raised to add a full basement, and new classrooms were added along with a pastor's office. The below photograph demonstrates how vegetation often obscures the object being photographed in the "present" pictures in this book. (Past, WCM 12,383.)

At the intersection of Third Avenue and Walnut Street stood a Catholic church on the left and a Baptist church on the right. The historic Rice-Gates House is on the right at 308 SE Walnut Street. The house on the left is at 272 SE Walnut Street; it was built in 1910 and still looks much like it did in its early years. Both churches are now gone from their respective corners. The new Catholic church is still on the same block, just north on the corner of Third Avenue and Oak Street. (Past, WCM 15,419.)

Here are the two Catholic churches on Third Avenue. The older building—with the distinctive striped cap on the tower—was on the southern end of the block, while the modern St. Matthew's Church (built in 1965) is at 447 S. Third Avenue on the northern end of the same block at the corner of Third Avenue and Oak Street. (Past, WCM 462.)

The First Baptist Church on the northwest corner of Second Avenue and Lincoln Street was dedicated in 1922. The 1912 Sanborn map shows two large greenhouses at that corner. However, the 1921 map shows the greenhouses not there anymore, creating an empty space for the Baptist church. A major remodeling effort was undertaken on the 1922 church that resulted in the present configuration of the church at the same corner, with an address of 177 E. Lincoln Street. (Past, WCM 26,010.)

First Baptist Church   Hillsboro, Oregon

The Christian Church at the southeast corner of Third Avenue and Baseline Street is shown above. A small, one-story business center is visible across Third Avenue in both images. Below, the shopping center that replaced the church is fenced off in preparation for demolition in the summer of 2022. (Past, WCM 482.)

The United Methodist Church is shown at Third Avenue and Washington Street. The church sat on the northwest corner across Third Avenue from the Oregon Electric Railway depot. The church is long gone, and that corner is now a parking lot for the Faber building. (Past, WCM 484.)

Hillsboro's United Methodist Church is now at 168 NE Eighth Avenue and has changed little since it was constructed in 1950. It was built to replace the church at Third Avenue and Washington Street. (Past, author's collection.)

The old Evangelical Church was on the southeast corner of Fifth Avenue and Fir Street (Walnut Street). There is now a private home at that corner location. (Past, WCM 471.)

SCHOOLS AND CHURCHES

At left is the First Congregational Church, at the northwest corner of Fifth Avenue and Main Street, as it looked in 1908. The church was severely damaged by the Columbus Day storm in 1962. The damaged building was razed, and a new church was built on the same spot with an address of 494 E. Main Street. The new sanctuary was dedicated in 1965. (Past, WCM 481.)

The 1912 photograph at right shows the Christian Church on the northeast corner of Third Avenue and Baseline Street. The church's entrance faced Third Avenue. The picture was taken by Oliver Manford Pope, a well-known photographer in Hillsboro and Forest Grove. The corner is now occupied by a store that specializes in car batteries. (Past, WCM 476.)

CHAPTER 4

HOMES

John Willis Masters made a home in Hillsboro. There is a large barn at the rear of it. Masters was born near Orenco in 1845. He was listed as a farmer in the 1900 census and as a merchant in 1910. (WCM 759.)

The Malcolm McDonald home was built in 1912 at 7250 NE Birch Street in Orenco Woods Nature Park. McDonald was president of the Oregon Nursery Company (Orenco). The McDonald home is currently owned by the City of Hillsboro. The city is hoping to obtain funding to renovate it and take down the fencing so it can be opened back up to the public. (Past, WCM 940.)

Archibald McGill, vice president of the Oregon Nursery Company, had this Craftsman-style home built in 1907. McGill's home was a short distance from the Malcolm McDonald home. The Orenco office was also built in the Craftsman style. All three of these buildings were connected by a wooden boardwalk. Today, McGill's home at 6832 NE Cherry Drive is surrounded by numerous large apartment complexes. (Past, WCM 943.)

The Rice-Gates house at 308 SE Walnut Street was built in 1890 by William Rice, an attorney from New Jersey. Henry Gates was a well-known railroad man who oversaw the construction of hundreds of miles of railways in Oregon and California. Gates bought the house from Rice in 1895. Walnut Street was originally named Fir Street, as evidenced by the bronze letters (seen in the inset below) set in the sidewalk on the corner of Walnut Street and Third Avenue. (Past, WCM 3,685.)

The Charles Tozier family home is shown below in 1912. The house was on the north side of Baseline Street between Third and Fourth Avenues. It was adjacent to the Christian Church on the corner of Third Avenue and Baseline Street near where the driveway is seen above. The maple trees were planted by Charles Tozier in 1872. The Tozier house was torn down, and now only one dead maple remains. (Past, WCM 1,386.)

The home at 173 NE Third Avenue, pictured below with a man standing on the sidewalk in front, was built by W.H. Connell in 1907–1909. He sold it to William Donelson in 1909, a famous undertaker in Hillsboro who also bought the large Queen Anne home next door, which he converted into a funeral home. Between the two was a water tower. The Donelson house is now home to Decadent Creations, a bakery. (Past, WCM 30,430.)

HOMES

Hillsboro doctor Francis Alonzo Bailey (1849–1930) made his home on the southwest corner of Second Avenue and Baseline Street. His son Earl Bailey used the home at 219 E. Baseline Street as an ice cream parlor in the 1950s. The home was torn down in 1966. A shopping center now occupies that corner lot. (Past, WCM 2,959.)

No. 12 RESIDENCE STREET HILLSBORO ORE.

These images show the intersection of Fourth Avenue and Jackson Street. The homes on the immediate left and right have changed little in the time between these two photographs. The most obvious differences are the paved streets and that the intersection now has lined crosswalks. Another difference is the large number of trees seen below. (Past, WCM 15,265.)

Built in 1866, the Robert Imbrie home is shown below in an 1892 photograph taken by Avery Crandall, son of Washington County judge Rudolph Crandall. The Imbrie house is now used as one of the many McMenamins restaurants in the county. The restaurant in the Imbrie building is known as the Cornelius Pass Roadhouse at 4045 Cornelius Pass Road. Over the years, few alterations have been made to the front exterior of the building. (Past, WCM 867.)

The Heidel house was built in 1905 as a private home. In 1966, it was purchased by the Washington County Historical Society and became the location of the Washington County Museum, as indicated by the sign hanging on the front porch. The museum moved out of this 641 E. Main Street location to its new home at the Portland Community College's Rock Creek campus in 1982. The Main Street Apartments now occupy the former Heidel house. (Past, Five Oaks Museum.)

CHAPTER 5

COMMERCE

Located at 171 SE Second Avenue, on the west side of Second Avenue between Main Street and Washington Street, was the Portland Electric Power (PEP) business office. PEP was the name used by the Portland General Electric Company in the 1930s and 1940s. The company was reorganized in 1948 and changed its name to Portland General Electric (PGE). (Oregon Historical Society.)

The above photograph shows the Portland General Electric business office at 171 SE Second Avenue, one building up from the corner. The Pythian Building is just up the street, and the railroad tracks along Washington Street are visible at bottom. The brightly colored building on the corner below is home to the Hillsboro Artists' Regional Theatre (HART). The railway tracks of the TriMet Blue Line run across the bottom of the modern image. Trees now obscure most of the buildings on the left side of the block. (Past, WCM 13,263.)

The Hillsboro City Water and Light Works tower was built in 1891 near the center of the block just north of courthouse square. It was razed in 1914 after more than 20 years of service. The young lady in the modern image is standing about where the three men stood in the original photograph. The parking lot is behind the First Baptist Church and is reserved for church personnel and employees of the Hillsboro Civic Center. (Past, WCM 1,259.)

The Carnation Company milk condensing plant was at 669 S. First Avenue just south of the railroad tracks. In 1948, the Carnation Company converted the plant from producing condensed milk to making Friskies brand dog food. For a short time, the building was called Albers; the Albers Milling Company was a division of Carnation, and Albers canned the Friskies dog food. The plant closed, and the building is now home to numerous small businesses. (Past, WCM 13,877.)

The above aerial photograph from 1979 shows the first building at Intel's Hawthorne Farm campus. Cornell Road cuts diagonally across the top. The six round structures off the sides of that first building are still visible in the recent satellite view of the expanded campus below. (Past, WCM 18,395.)

The Climax Mill on Second Avenue milled flour. It was on the south end of Second Avenue, which was cut in half by the railroad tracks, so Second Avenue had a northern half and a southern half. Below, Second Avenue is shown leading away from the railroad tracks with a row of trees and a small apartment complex on the property at left where the Climax Mill once stood. (Past, WCM 1,034.)

At the northwest corner of Second Avenue and Baseline Street was a Safeway grocery store with its front entrance facing Second Avenue. After Safeway closed, the building was used for the Selfridge furniture store, which put the large arch over the relocated front entrance. The building at 175 SE Baseline Street is now home to a Mattress MegaStore. (Past, WCM 14,205.)

Hamby Chevrolet opened in 1946 at its downtown Hillsboro location at 172 S. First Avenue. The corner at W. Washington Street and S. First Avenue was used to show off the latest Chevy pickups.

That same corner is now a parking lot adjacent to the Hillsboro Civic Center building. (Past, WCM 13,995.)

The Hamby family opened a new Chevrolet dealership at 1084 Oak Street in the 1960s. Car dealers do not want trees on the property (to preclude material dropping onto the cars). Over the years, ownership of the dealership on Oak Street changed, and it became known as Bruce's Chevrolet and then Dick's Chevrolet. As of January 2022, the name on the sign was Tonkin. (Past, WCM 13,996.)

Wess Hebron opened his barbershop at 453 E. Baseline Street in 1960. He was known for many firsts in the barbering world—not only in Hillsboro but across the nation. He was the first to take appointments and the first to take credit cards, among even more firsts. He often had a popcorn machine set up on the sidewalk. The small concrete building that comes right to the sidewalk is still there, but the barbershop is long gone, with Hebron cutting his last hair there in 1997. (Past, WCM 13,807.)

The Art Deco Hill Theater, built in 1937 on Third Avenue, is shown with a long line of people queuing up to buy tickets to a double bill of *The Curse of Frankenstein* and *X the Unknown*. *The Curse of Frankenstein* was released in 1957. The theater and the adjacent florist shop are now home to the Hill Theater Antique Mall at 127 NE Third Avenue. (Past, WCM 14,198.)

Originally, the southwest corner of Third Avenue and Lincoln Street was the site for a Queen Anne–style home. William Donelson bought the home and converted it to a funeral parlor, which explains the hearse parked out front in the below photograph. In 1941, the original structure was torn down, and a more modern rectangular building was erected to serve as the funeral home. The building was abandoned as a mortuary in 2008. The 1941 building is now home to the Collective Market. (Past, WCM 284.)

The Commercial Hotel on the left sat at the intersection of Washington Street and Second Avenue on the northwest corner until it was destroyed by a fire in January 1912. A livery stable was across the street just beyond where the three children are posing above. In the 19th and early 20th centuries, most hotels had a livery stable nearby. The corner where the Commercial Hotel once sat is now the site of the brightly colored HART building. (Past, WCM 1,728.)

This house at 222 S. Ninth Avenue was used as a place of business for a short time in the late 1950s. It was called the Cub Hill Mop & Specialty Company and was owned by Gustaf Heinrich Albert Blunck, born in Germany in 1895. Mops were the main item manufactured here. The home was demolished, and the location is currently a construction site. (Past, WCM 14,459.)

CHAPTER

6

TRANSPORTATION

This wagon is stuck in the mud on Main Street around 1911. The Tualatin Hotel is directly behind it. In an attempt to remedy the problem of muddy streets, wooden planks were installed on portions of Main Street and Second Avenue in the heart of Hillsboro's downtown business district. It was not until the early years of the 20th century—when asphalt started to be used to pave streets and roads—that people were finally saved from getting stuck in the mud. (WCM 13,469.)

To combat the muddy streets in downtown Hillsboro, thick wooden planks were installed on portions of Main Street and Second Avenue. The below image looks north and shows the planks being installed on Second Avenue. Luckily, asphalt paving came along in the first decades of the 20th century and provided a much better solution than the planks. Above, the modern building with the black awning is near where the meat market is seen below. (Past, WCM 1,180.)

Above, three men stand on the sidewalk outside the corner drugstore. The view is south down Second Avenue, which is covered in wooden planks. Below, the drugstore has been replaced with a bank building, which is pictured in the process of being renovated to house four new restaurants. The wooden street and sidewalks have been replaced with asphalt and concrete. (Past, WCM 1,721.)

On Baseline Street between Hillsboro and Cornelius, the road had to cross Dairy Creek, which formed the western boundary of Hillsboro. A wooden bridge built to make the crossing was called Long Bridge. At the eastern end of the bridge, on the north side of the road, is Hillsboro's Pioneer Cemetery. The photograph below shows that the original wooden guardrails have been replaced with concrete and aluminum. (Past, author's collection.)

Below, a section of the 1905 bridge at Jackson Bottom is shown crossing the Tualatin River just south of town. Because the city dumped human waste directly into the river, there was an unpleasant odor. Many complaints were made, and the wooden bridge was purposefully burned in 1921. Then, a more modern bridge replaced it. In the 1964 image at left, the southern section of the newer bridge is underwater during a flood. (Past, WCM 204.)

The depot building for the Oregon Electric Railway was on the north side of Washington Street between Third and Fourth Avenues. Below, a boxcar is sitting on a siding that ran in front of the depot. The old depot building was blown down during the Columbus Day storm in 1962. The TriMet transfer station, with the Hillsboro Blue Line building, was constructed on the same location where the old depot once stood. Service began in 1998. (Past, WCM 1,723.)

TRANSPORTATION

In 1900, a form of asphalt called bitulithic pavement was patented. These two images show the installation of pavement in the past and in the present; the term "macadamizing" was once used to describe this process. The modern asphalt-laying operation is similar to the one shown in the 1911 image above, except no real horses were used to provide "horsepower." (Past, WCM 11,869; present, FreeForm.com.)

In the decades after World War II, it seemed almost every corner contained a full-service gas station. Full service meant that an employee would pump the gas and clean the windshield, along with checking the tire pressure, radiator water level, and oil. Oregon banned full-service gas pumping in 1951. The site at 275 E. Baseline is now home to a Shell gas station; instead of a service bay, it has a convenience store. (Past, WCM 14,253.)

INDEX

DISCOVER THOUSANDS OF LOCAL HISTORY BOOKS FEATURING MILLIONS OF VINTAGE IMAGES

Arcadia Publishing, the leading local history publisher in the United States, is committed to making history accessible and meaningful through publishing books that celebrate and preserve the heritage of America's people and places.

Find more books like this at
www.arcadiapublishing.com

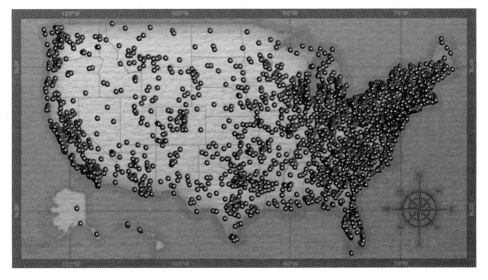

Search for your hometown history, your old stomping grounds, and even your favorite sports team.

Consistent with our mission to preserve history on a local level, this book was printed in South Carolina on American-made paper and manufactured entirely in the United States. Products carrying the accredited Forest Stewardship Council (FSC) label are printed on 100 percent FSC-certified paper.

MADE IN THE